T0198849

Somewhere Between Dreams and Memories

Miriam Susan Carstons

SOMEWHERE BETWEEN DREAMS AND MEMORIES

iUniverse books may be ordered through booksellers or by contacting:

iUniverse
1663 Liberty Drive
Bloomington, IN 47403
www.iuniverse.com
1-800-Authors (1-800-288-4677)

ISBN: 978-1-4917-6890-7 (sc)
ISBN: 978-1-4917-6889-1 (e)

Library of Congress Control Number: 2015909479

Print information available on the last page.

iUniverse rev. date: 01/05/2016

To Sue Bee – who for part of the journey,
came along for the ride.

Contents

Acknowledgments

This would not have been possible without ShirleyMacLaine.com. A heartfelt thank you goes out to Shirley MacLaine and Brit Elders for creating and maintaining this wonderful forum for independent expression.

I. Introduction

In my mid twenties, I had a dream one night that I was a baby in a crib, crying, and my mother came to get me. She brought me into the kitchen and sat me on her lap so that I was facing my aunt, who was standing pouring coffee for my mom and herself. The dream ended as my aunt was sitting back down and they were continuing their conversation.

The next morning, I called my mother and told her about this dream. It was such a vivid dream that I felt compelled to tell her where the crib was, where a dresser was, where an open window was, how a hot, muggy breeze was lifting a sheer white curtain. I also described where everything was in the kitchen.

She was amazed. She told me it wasn't a dream. I was about eighteen months old, and we were living with my aunt, and we all moved shortly after that, and none of us ever went back.

Some years later, in 2003, I underwent some regression therapy, and while under hypnosis, once again the same phenomenon occurred. My repressed memories appeared before me like dreams.

And now as I get older, even my conscious memories of this life appear like dreams when I look back at them. Take a look at one of your memories; is it not like a dream now?

Experiences like this have created a small tear in the fabric of time-space for me. If some dreams can be memories of moments from this life, could some dreams harbor bits and pieces of our past lives? It's something I ponder with every dream.

II. Humble Insights during Meditation

Electrons

It's in our DNA—
how we change
from particles to waves
when someone is watching.

Crossing Over

All extremes cross over, it seems.
Travelling at the speed of light, one is still.
And dry ice is so cold that it crosses over into hot.
With profound sorrow, there is sometimes laughter.
With intense joy, there are sometimes tears.
As I contemplate this, there's a hint here
with regard to transcending barriers.
But it seems the highest octaves of sound
cannot be heard as they cross over into silence.

Or can they?

In God's Image

Perhaps initially it's a thought propelled
from out of some conscious, wide-awake, invisible force
that sets the universe into action.
And as the cosmos begins to swirl,
molecules are drawn together into a kind of vortex,
until packed so tightly, they become matter.

In Genesis chapter 1,
"something greater than ourselves"
alludes to how it's done—
as if spirit opens its eyes
and eternity arrives
wrapped in a moment.

When I close my eyes, where am I? I'm still there, but where?
There's a hint there.

The Heart of the Moment

Deep within the dark abyss of my self
on a bridge between my breaths,
I happened upon a moment.
And as it caught me by surprise,
from the center of my eye,
I became mesmerized
as it drew me to itself like a magnet.

I don't know how long I lingered there,
for time and space did not exist,
But I will tell you this:
Love is all there is …
in the heart of a moment.

III. Lady of the Highlands

The Potion

She walks through the forest barefoot
in search of just the right herbs, the right roots—
the ones with just the right colors,
just the right scents—
and gathering them all together into her basket,
she carries them all the way home.

Once inside her quaint little cottage,
one can hear the lovely melody she sings
as she conjures up her powerful potion
and gives it its powerful name.

She calls it Imagination, and as she stirs it,
she thinks of all the magic it will bring.

Wild Horses

Drawn by the soothing rhythm of her drum,
from the four directions they did come,
just to graze near her beneath the setting sun—
a herd of wild horses.

And when she rose to walk away,
the herd moved with her, to her dismay,
and they followed her all the way
until she would no longer let them.

"Shoo," she said. "Run and be free,
and stay away from the likes of me—
for they will break you and bring you to your knees.
Stay free, you beautiful wild horses."

And so off they ran across the plain,
but not too far from her do they ever stray.
She can see them grazing each and every day
on the edge of her horizon.

Familiar Wood

As he paced his mare through Familiar Wood,
the sun flickered through the trees.
The air was crisp,
and in the morning mist,
the sound of crunching leaves …
It felt good to be back in Familiar Wood,
though he wondered what lay in store.
Would she be welcoming him back with open arms,
or would she be slamming the door?
Oh … she was a fiery lass; he laughed.
Aye … she could be a bit of a shrew.
But though she be concealing what she was feeling,
he would always be seeing right through.
For there in her eyes, the truth did shine
that aye … she loved him too.

A Speck of Light

It seemed the mare had had a scare
and thrown him clear for a loop.
And when he came to
(with a gash on his head and a bit of dread),
there was absolutely nothing he could remember.
He did not know where he was, why he was, or who he was.
He did not know where he had been or where he was going.
It was as if he was in a now abyss, and it was in this now
that night had fallen.
In this ragged state, he made his way through the wood
on a narrow path, clinging desperately to
one branch and then another until at last he
discovered what he sensed was a clearing.
Pitch-black it was. Pitch-black.
But in this open space, there was a bit of grace,
for in the distance, a tiny light was swaying.
It was the strangest sight, this speck of light—
for it was dancing with the breeze.
"I must be daft," he laughed—but as he made his way closer,
glory be!
It was a woman, and she was holding up a lantern
so he could see! Not just any woman, mind
you. She was the woman in his dreams!
And in a flash, just before he collapsed,
he remembered everything!
A day would pass before he would wake and ask,
"How was it that she knew?"
She said the mare had found her way back, and by
the light of her lamp, she figured he would too.
"Aye," he said, "indeed I did, all the way back to you."

Follow the Yellow Brick Road

Which is the healing road?
Good witches know.
The path to healing starts with feeling
and then letting go.
And so while wishing us well,
they cast their spells as the river rises,
by tossing herbs and spices
into the river's flow.

Aye ... good witches know.

IV. Rapture

The Great Flood

I shall not be far from you
when the rains come,
knowing that soon after
we shall dance in the sun.
In a glistening meadow,
to you my spirit will run
when the rain comes.

The Return of the Sun

And when the clouds departed,
the sun came out to play,
and the spirit rose up to greet it,
and it asked the sun that day:
"Why do I feel elated on the days you come to call?
What is it that I'm made of that makes me love you so?"
And the sun shone even brighter, for it knew the answer well:
"I am light, and you feel lighter
because you are light yourself."

A Healing Rain

Sun is stronger now.
Tears of joy from Father Sky.
Rainbows hug the clouds.

V. Wisdom of the Pond and the Trees

There in the Pond

Sometimes our thoughts
are like drops of morning dew
that fall from leaves into a still pond,
creating points of disturbance
from which tiny circles expand
until they touch and blend
into an ocean of meaning.
And when the surface of the pond
once again becomes calm,
only then do we begin to see
the whole reflection.

More in the Pond

It is only when the ice on the pond begins to melt
that the pond begins to sparkle.

Older Trees

It seems to me
that it's an older tree
that awakens in autumn
than the one that awakens in spring—
a more rounded,
grounded,
seasoned
thing
on its way to acquiring yet another ring.
Yes, a tree in the midst of autumn
is a profound thing indeed.

Winter's Night

These trees standing together in a
winter wonderland of white,
how beautifully they rise into the crisp night air,
with the snow on their limbs picturesquely,
their limbs trembling ever so slightly
in the subsiding winds …

One of God's gifts to them, I think,
and one of their gifts to us,
the graceful way in which they bare their winters.

Tending the Fire

It's an art to keep the fire in a hearth slowly burning,
to know how much to kindle and when to begin stirring,

creating just the right amount of space between the logs
so the fire can breathe, taking in all the oxygen it needs.

It also requires a minor education in woods—which
kinds burn fast and which kinds burn slowly,
the right synergetic combination that will set the hearth aglow,
like white birch and dark oak for example.

I can tend such a fire for hours during quiet times alone.

VI. Channeling Virginia

Sailing Home to Virginia

Within my mind, reflections dance across
the ocean's great expanse
while friend ships float on crystal seas
old with time, in reverie.
Slow-motion tide, emotion's force
sets the heart upon a course.
Enormous sails flap in the wind,
arousing spirits once again
to rise, to soar, to sense how great
these images are that time creates.

The Book of Stars

Funny how you, a complete stranger,
should remind me of that day so long ago when, all lit up,
he came strutting out onto the terrace still in his riding boots,
a day earlier than he was supposed to.
I recall how he held me there in his gaze.
His eyes were like an autumn meadow,
amber golden halos bursting out into fields of iridescent green,
fusing into the most vibrant shade of gray I'd ever seen.
Oh I swear, that man could make time
stand still right along with us,
before turning away to fix his gaze on the infinite sky.
We stood quiet for a moment until, as I watched him there,
he began to talk to the air and me at the same time.
"I brought cha something," he said. "Would you like to see?"
Well, I knew it was a book. He was always bringing me books.
Oh they'd come in different shapes and sizes, wrapped in
tissue paper of many colors, but it was always books.
"Here," he said. "Take a look."
"What's it about?" I asked as I unwrapped it.
"It's about the stars," he replied.
"It's so you'll know their names and where they are."
I recall as I turned the pages of that book, it
had the prettiest painted pictures, and I liked
it so much that I read it in no time at all.
And later that night, as I stood with him up on his mountain,
naming all the constellations I could find, I do declare
it was the sweetest distraction to watch his reaction
from the corner of my eye. Oh yes, that was a lovely night.

Sassafras

I am recalling the green leaves of our summers,
the way the light flickered through them
and how the sweet scent of sassafras did linger
in the dampness of those lazy mornings
when we would take to walking down your favorite paths,
naming birds, naming plants—a plethora of facts you loved
to share. And how just before nightfall, inhaling the air,
the scent of sassafras would always come back.
Summer mornings and evenings were always like that.

A Letter to Heaven

Dear Miss Abigail,
I'm writing this to you, though you will never receive this,
but I am saddened by the loss of your love,
just as I'm saddened by the loss of mine.
And even though my children will soon be freed,
and soon I too am going to be,
I find no comfort in freedom at this time.
I do declare, if I could just see them both standing there
conversing on the terrace, I'd gladly remain a slave forever.

Yonder on the Hill

I've been seeing a Union soldier this morning
standing on that hillside over yonder,
but I cannot tell if he is dead or alive because lately
I've taken to seeing apparitions, even where they are none.
I'm just a child I know... from some time long ago,
but lately I can never tell if I'm seeing
deep into a person's soul
or if that soul is all that's left returning
for something he's forgotten -
or even worse,
not wanting to leave something behind
that he can't take with him.
He stands there looking down over
the body of another soldier.
Shots fired and momma shouts "Child,
get away from that window!"
and as I watch that harmless Union soldier,
she rushes over and yanks me away by the arm.
It's that relentless grip I know so well
that negates my God-given free will
and I protest immediately. "But Momma there's no one there!
It's just some Union soul looking over
a body that might be his".
My words only serve to make her more
frantic as she draws me closer
and holds me tightly and I almost suffocate as she laments,
"Oh my sweet baby, this war has made you crazy;

will you EVER be normal again?! And
now she drags me with her
to that corner of refuge that she has
created with the turned-over table
that we used to eat on, that now protects us
from ghosts that cannot harm us that she insists are real.
Which one of us is crazy, I ask you? Which one?
And there we hide all day and night
and as the gunfire continues
Momma rocks herself and me until I fall asleep in her arms.
And in the morning, when I return to the window
in search of that Union soldier on the hillside -
though I can still see his body; the Union soldier is gone.

June 3, 1861 – Warrington, VA

I remember clearly after all the burying was done,
how we mothers, wives, sisters, and daughters
did gather up from our gardens the sweetest of flowers
in the brightest of colors—load up the wagons
and head for the graveyards.

I remember, with the bees buzzing and the flies swarming,
approaching, arriving, each of us dismounting,
gathering up our baskets, and below each tombstone
we placed at least ten flowers, and it took hours,
like they took ours—some of them slowly.

It was like tending to a field with seeds needing planting,
drops of perspiration and tears falling
slowly to the ground in the hot sun.

Some might say the war against the South was won,
but if you lost your father, your brother, your husband,
your son, I tell you … it matters not what side you were on.
Nothing was won.

But across the great expanse of our graveyards,
after all the decorating was done and we stood remembering
our fathers, brothers, husbands, sons,
loss became a sweet fragrance, and our valleys of death
beautiful gardens to gaze upon.

VII. On the Shores of an Ethereal Sea

Eternity

She was like a beautiful island that
held his gaze in the distance
as he sailed slowly 'cross her endless sea,
and he was like a mighty ship that she
watched in the distance, drifting, with its sails
flapping in the crisp, cool breeze,
and in the dancing reflections of the waters between them,
they glimpsed eternity.

Sand Castles

Come sit before the sea
and build sandcastles with me.
We'll build them to the sky
and then watch the clouds drift by
from the inside.

We'll set our inner children free,
and we'll let them play and be
as we watch them gleefully
from the inside.

We'll leave their footprints in the sand,
the tiny footprints we once had.
We'll laugh, and we'll be glad
from the inside.

Wishes

The crescent moon is smiling tonight,
and as the tide fills the night air with wishes,
the cool, wet sands conspire with it
to soothe our barefoot souls.

Listening to Her Breathing

Alone on the brink of night,
on the edge of twilight,
with the ebb tide peacefully
wishing up to shore,
pulling away slowly,
wishing gently up once more,
it's as if Mother Earth is sleeping,
and I'm listening to her breathing.
Soothes me to the core.

Tides Within

Many times have you moved
the ocean in me
like the moon moves the sea,
without touching.

And many times it has been
on the edge of your shores,
awakening once more
that my ocean has come rushing.

Longing

What is longing but an ocean of emotion
stretching out as far as thou can see,
rushing all the way back to thee.
And oh … if only longing were an entity;
how sweet would that be.

Dusk Dawning

What truths are there for me and you
as day and night give way in tune
to each other.
The setting sun, the rising moon,
the sparkling stars that shine so true,
that disappear and break into
the dawning hues of sunlight.
Upon the earth the morning dew,
the mountain mist that rises too,
to greet the sky as down below
upon the shores, the rising tides come rushing
till evening's light draws near, and then
the tide begins to ebb again
just before we set again ... to dreaming.

VIII. Japan

Love and Honor

The wind honors the chimes;
the chimes love the wind.
Love and honor are very delicate things;
creates a tingle.

The Ojii-san by Tama River

I remember bike riding with my friends
on a dirt path one day …
along the pristine, clean, crystal-
clear waters of the Tama River.
We were kids in a foreign land exploring,
hollering out to each other and laughing
as we rode this narrow dirt path.

Ojii-san stood across the river,
dressed in navy blue kimono
with his hands behind his back—
like a statue … just staring out on the water.

He looked up slowly, and it was clear
we had disturbed the silence,
but Ojii-san didn't seem to mind;
he smiled as we passed at our childish chatter.

Something about the old man intrigued me,
enough to make me look back—
but when I did, he was gone.

After all these years, today I remember the Ojii-san
whose path we crossed for just one moment.
Does he ever remember the same moment?
Did he even exist?

Encounter

Geisha waits on bridge,
wrapped up in bright kimono,
obi for a bow.

Samurai draws near.
His eyes steadfast upon her,
she bows … rising slow.

Cherry blossoms fall
down gently all around her
like white, scented snow.

Hearts begin to pound.
Taken by such beauty, he …
turns and lets her go.

A stag now grazing
looks up. Instinct takes over!
Over there—a doe!

Old Haunts

The tingling of faraway chimes,
floating …
The bonsai tree I used to climb,
growing …
The bridge I crossed in Nikko,
knowing …
I would never be the same.

Hanabi

Long ago on a bridge called Kokoru,
near the Miosame River,
her kimono colors bright,
orange blossom, green tea rose,
my rising sun took flight.
With passion wrapped in love's embrace,
on wings that split the night,
my geisha gave her heart to me
as I, too, gave her mine.
Stars bursting in the sky …

The Temple Gong

To the still pond that trembles with joy,
it is the sweet noise of awakening,
and to the cherry blossom shaken from the tree
that floats on the breeze,
it is the sweet song of liberation.
And to the one who has the ear
to follow the sound until it disappears,
it is a path to realization.

Impending Winter

Soon the tall green pines of Fujiyama shall begin
to sway with longing for their mistress snow.
And soon, without warning, she shall come to rest upon
their limbs in the moonlight and set them all aglow.

IX. The Heartlands of the Poet

The Truer Self

It's a truer self that flows from the pen
as it loops with ease into eyes that slide into seas
of thoughts and sentiments the self is out to convey.
A trail is blazed, the message enhanced
by lines rising and falling like waves upon the sand.
The ink is damp; our marks are made,
and no two scripts are quite the same.

4:00 a.m.

It's in the wee hours of morning,
in the quiet of night,
when in such sweet serenity
I am inspired to write
of emotions and notions
that come into light,
an ocean of potions
I drink with delight.
Sometimes I can see myself
in some long-ago life
writing with quill
by lantern's light—
there in the darkness,
with my thoughts taking flight,
staining the parchment
until morning's light.

Creative Spark

What is music
but a dream
that turns emotions into notes
that rise and fall
and rise again
to tell it all
without telling.

What is a painting
but a scheme
to draw the seen
and the unseen
into one eternal moment
unfolding.

And what is poetry
but a line
that extends from the heart
up to the mind
that awakens it
by adding rhyme
to all its linear reason.

Our Days and Nights at the Aura Cafe

I do so recall the way our words floated into one another's,
melting into such a sweet collective essence,
rising high above the mire, serving to inspire us all
to fall madly in love with each other.
It was a trance in which we effortlessly danced
while hanging on to every word.

Where the Poets Go

There is a place between the lines
where the poets go,
where beauty rises from the mist
and the rivers flow
into oceans of notions
that bloom and grow
into beautiful gardens of meaning.

Upon entering these garden gates,
perhaps by chance, perhaps through fate,
they become one with other poets,
all engaged in a kind of collective dreaming.

No poet writes alone,
for inspiration is a divine gift that flows
from this land of collective dreaming
into beautiful gardens of meaning.

Years Later

I remember you,
a poet back then ...
(much like myself)
molding hard reality into something soft and light.
How we tripped the light fandango;
how we fought the good fight.

X. Some Themes Universal

Love and Fear

Good-bye says the stranger.
Hello says the friend.
So long is a journey,
a journey without end.
Fear is the stranger;
the friend, a love that dwells.
And the thread that binds the two
is as old as time itself.
A leaf that is picked
from a tree ripe with age,
A book that still beckons you
to turn another page.
Go back where the music
can be heard outside the door,
and the telephone rings twice,
breaking the silence once more;
on a road that lies quiet,
lined with trees on either side,
where a heart beats ever gently
with a love that never dies.

Burning Bridges

It seems it is inevitable
that a heart will surely close,
for where there is an angry storm,
dampness long after dwells.
And dampness fed by distant winds
will freeze the sweetest dream,
and bitter cold will never let
the warmth in heart be free.
Locked within, the miracles
await a glimmering chance—
the coming of the summer song
forgotten with the past.
And still we gaze out helplessly
to watch the bridges burn.
Let not the fire touch our hearts;
it seems we never learn.
My God, we never learn.

Candle in the Window

A candle in the window,
a torch within my heart.
A flame that flickers brightly
illuminates the dark.
In the center of that brightness,
shades of orange, red, and blue
seduce me in the darkness;
makes me remember you.
How our eyes were like an ocean
we dove into with a gaze.
And there we swam, suspended
in eternity's embrace—
until I reached the shoreline.
I would blink, and you'd be gone,
as the candle quivered lightly,
as it melted into dawn.

XI. Channeling Clare

Recipe for Healing

Go inside
and get a bucket
and place it right here.
Then, stand right beside it
with all of your tears.
Let the rain fall
from the sky
and let the rain fall
from your eyes at will
until that bucket is filled.
Then go find a garden. Go.
And with your tears
mixed with God's tears,
help something grow.

E-motion

When we cry—
don't you know that
our tears fall into rivers
that flow into oceans
that rush up to greet us
and then pull away?
Don't you know
that we cry with the eagles,
we cry with the seagulls
along the shorelines
of a brand-new day?
And don't you know
that when our hearts are broken,
the heavens open
so that we may know joy
in the same way—
with tears that fall into rivers
and flow into oceans
that rush up to greet us
and then pull away.

Awakening

Oh, sweet solitary soul—
because you listen,
the birds sing songs for you,
and the river glistens
because you see.
And because you smell them,
the grasses are fragrant,
and because you taste it,
the apple is sweet.
It is the essence
of your very presence
that awakens every sentient thing.

John of God

Metaphysically,
it's like open-heart surgery—
when someone touches your heart.

A Simple Truth

A heart must ache before it can break
wide open with love's true expression.
It's a prerequisite, it seems;
before the dream, there must be longing.

So long with me—
for it's the tree's longing for the sun
that makes it burst with all its colors.
And it's the spirit longing for itself
that makes it run to another
to express every nuance of wonder that it feels.

XII. Tantric Dreams

Opening Night

A sound,
like the leaves
of a thousand trees rustling …
The flutter
of a thousand butterflies …
A rush
of clouds swiftly passing …
Something like the sun bursting
through the sky …
Rain drops
like a curtain in stages—
mist first, then teeming with crowds
that gather, tossing roses at the feet of Devi
while Shiva lovingly looks on.

Baring All

What passion stirs from raw emotion,
as if in baring such tender wounds,
we step out of the trappings
of our own apprehensions,
allowing them to fall to the floor.
And with spirits exposed
and hearts wide open,
we are free to love—
to truly love
once more.

Just Before Entering

I see your cottage in my mind,
with love's inspiration deep inside,
and love, having searched for it far and wide,
longing to be taken all the way inside,
now stands at the doorway knocking.

Cosmic Love

As destiny and fate
converse with the stars at night,
inspiring the spirit of imagination,

and Mother Earth
conspires with delight
to stir that spirit into action and manifestation,

while we travel the back roads of our minds
seeking transcendence and illumination,

stumbling upon those roads
that lead to higher consciousness and
deeper comprehension,

the divine feminine and masculine
are dancing in the light with joyful anticipation.

Stardust

Give me wings.
Let me fly.
Let me soar across the sky.
Wrap me up in midnight blue.
Let me touch the crescent moon.
Take me higher,
all the way,
breaking through the Milky Way
to a million twinkling stars,
and then tell me who we are.
Tell me.

Enlightenment

Melting ice trickles
into sparkling streams of consciousness,
skipping over rocks.
Tickled by the splashes
on her eyelashes;
the inner child laughs.

XIII. Seasonal Renderings

Spring

Why do they call it spring?
Is it because every single thing
springs into action?
And even the saddest thing … is suddenly transformed
by the poet into the sweetest rhapsody,
by the musician into the sweetest melody,
and by the magician into pure alchemy.
Even the painter's brush upon the canvas
transforms all the madness into a beautiful garden.
Oh how wonderful is spring.

Autumn's Ballet

Autumn arrives today with its cool, crisp winds,
lifting the particles of summer
like a Tibetan sand painting,
right up into the air—
and with both of them there,
just before summer gets carried away,
I watch them dance together in autumn's ballet.

Mabon's Muse

A part of myself that is lost in summer
can be found in autumn,
wandering thru the countryside
down an ethereal path
that leads all the way back to my heart,
as if the autumn breeze that sets the trees
to releasing what is deep inside of them
simultaneously awakens me to what is deep in me.
Autumn starts,
and suddenly grace appears
on the steps of my heart with the key.
It's such a sweet affinity.

Late Bloomers

In the book of seasons,
there are certain flowers in the sun
that start to bloom when the rest are done.
And drawn together by each one
are the butterflies that come
to flit and light upon them.

No one knows the reason,
but just as the trees
start to turn colors and release
all of their leaves,
the Japanese anemones (a-nem-O-knees)
bloom in perfect harmony
with greenery all around them.

For some strange, unknown reason,
with summer in her final stage,
the asters bloom with Russian sage,
and goldenrods become the rage
as Mother Nature turns the page
to autumn.

When He Was Spring and She Was Autumn

She was autumn, he was spring,
drawn together by the myriad things
that they could see
in their seasons' renderings.
He loved the many colors of her leaves;
she loved his buds upon the trees.
He loved the way that she released—
and she ... his way of bursting wide open.
She loved the shade that he gave—
and he ... the blanket that she made.
Each had a special way
of awakening the other.
Time did pass; the seasons changed;
their lives tossed and rearranged.
But even time could not erase
the essence of that time and space
when he was spring and she was autumn.

Seasons of My Life

I have fallen with the leaves in autumn,
taken flight with the birds in spring,
sat before the embers burning in the hearth
of my winter's dream,
and spent a thousand summers
awakening.

XIV. Visions

A Tear in the Fabric

A canary-yellow balloon
rises high into a clear blue sky.
A toddler in a stroller cries,
tears in her eyes,
her arms reaching for it in the sky.
My balloon!

And it begins—
a tiny tear in the fabric of innocence.

The Panoramic View

Growing old is like climbing a mountain.
The journey, at first sublime,
becomes arduous and exhausting—
hard on the mind and body
as we continue to climb.
But the higher we go,
as we reach each plateau,
one's vision expands.
And, man oh man,
how much more breathtaking
becomes the horizon.

Mountain Peak

Quiet is the dawn.
Sun yawns and then it stretches.
Seven colors fill the sky.

The Art of Being

Oh to soar like an eagle
as it crosses the great abyss—
to come to rest on a mountain peak
where the only sound is the wind—
and to be still there for a while
before taking off again.
Oh to glide on the air's current
as it caresses my belly and back;
to exist only for the sake of existence
without even knowing that.

Mediocrity and Greatness

In the book of ages,
as you turn the pages,
time and time again
you will find them there,
upon the bridge of realization,
on the brink of being lovers.
Mediocrity and greatness;
walking hand and hand,

in the heart of every woman,
in the heart of every man.

XV. Life after Life

Ancient Souls

Come sit with me by the fire
and warm yourself from the cold.
We'll wrap ourselves in a blanket
and wait for the tale to be told.
We'll stare into the fire
and watch it all unfold
all by itself, all by itself.

Youth

Do you remember when we were new,
like morning's dew
resting on tender leaves,
shimmering in the sunlight,
trembling in the breeze?
Do you remember when we were this:
canyon's echo,
mountain's mist?
Remember when we were bliss.

Chasing Hats in Avignon

Ode to the mistral of Avignon;
in days of old, along the Rhone,
when hats would fly as we did stroll
into the sky, and off we'd go—
chasing hats in Avignon.

Ode to the mistral of Avignon;
home of the seven sainted popes
in swirling, whirling, flowing robes—
they chased their hats in Avignon.

Ode to the mistral of Avignon;
for once, we too did call it home.
We frolicked there without a care;
sound of laughter in the air—
chasing hats in Avignon.

The Promise

Returning to him,
floating ethereally on the winds of time,
red velvet, cream lace falling from her
body gently to the ground.
Eyes, ice blue, melting—
beckoning him to come warm her.
He draws her to his chest,
and in love's passionate embrace,
she swears she'll never leave him.

Later … much later … she dies in his arms.

Déjà Vu

As the trees turned
with their golden leaves
to face a charcoal-gray sky,
two lovers turned with them
to gaze into each other's eyes.

"I want you to remember," said she,
as the sun came bursting through the sky.
"Do or die, I will always love you—
and because we met in autumn,
I will always love autumn too."

And so it came to pass
that they came to pass,
and then they came again.

And upon meeting for the first time
in the autumn of another life,
he asked, while gazing intently at her face:
"Why do I feel like I know you from some place?"

And with the leaves turning colors all around them,
she replied,
"I don't know, but don't you just love autumn?"
And the sun came bursting through the sky.

Metamorphosis

What if
dying and being born happen simultaneously?
What if, as we're dying,
the veils of time and space drop,
and we, no longer being confined,
become everything at once,
become pure consciousness
for that split second that is eternity
before returning once again,
one soul leaving one being for the other,
two beings morphing into each other
heading for the same light
at the end of the same tunnel
until—whack! A baby cries, and it's you or it's me.

Am I dreaming, or could it be a memory?

Universal Highway

I recall the light
at the end of the tunnel
driving out of the darkness
breaking through …
brand spanking new
into the bright sunshine.
The road winds around lines
of trees on both sides,
rushing swiftly past me
as if they've someplace to be,
some space behind me.
The warm air rushing in
through the window
like an old friend
running fingers through my hair,
and once again I am there
on that universal highway
travelling deep within,
that I might once again,
dare to share
all that unfolds before me.
And it occurs to me
that I will never run out of words to say
nor roads to take back to the ones I love.
In days of new, our days of old shall unfold too,
to show me the way back to them.

Printed in the United States
By Bookmasters